# BARBAROUS NIGHTS

Federico García Lorca

# BARBAROUS NIGHTS
Legends and Plays from The Little Theater

Translated by

Christopher Sawyer-Lauçanno

CITY LIGHTS BOOKS
San Francisco

Cover art: Federico García Lorca
Design by John Miller/Black and White Design

Library of Congress Cataloging-in-Publication Data

García Lorca, Federico, 1898-1936.
    [Selections, English, 1991]
    Barbarous nights : legends & plays / by Federico García
    Lorca ; translated from the Spanish by Christopher
    Sawyer-Lauçanno
        p.   cm.
    ISBN 0-87286-257-7 ; $9.95
    I. Title.
PQ6613.A763A6   1991
868'.6209--dc20                                        91-10332
                                                          CIP

City Lights Books are available to bookstores through our primary
distributor: Subterranean Company. P.O. Box 168, 265 S. 5th St.,
Monroe, OR 97456. 541-847-5274. Toll-free orders 800-274-7826.
FAX 541-847-6018. Our books are also available through library
jobbers and regional distributors. For personal orders and catalogs,
please write to City Lights Books, 261 Columbus Avenue,
San Francisco, CA 94133.

CITY LIGHTS BOOKS are edited by Lawrence Ferlinghetti and
Nancy J. Peters and published at the City Lights Bookstore,
261 Columbus Avenue, San Francisco, CA 94133.

*This translation is for my mother, Anne García, who first read me Lorca, whose passion for poetry first inspired my own.*

# CONTENTS

# INTRODUCTION

The works in this volume, with one possible exception, all date from between 1925 and 1928, an enormously productive period in Lorca's life, a time of formative experimentation in which the poet made his first real forays into the avant-garde. Although these works are integral to Lorca's development and indeed foreshadowed such major achievements as *Poet in New York* and a number of the more experimental plays, particularly *Así que pasen cinco años* (*If Five Years Pass*) and *The Public*, they have been largely ignored, even by critics, and are barely known to readers, including those in the Spanish-speaking world. This is unfortunate, for aside from being major markers in Lorca's artistic career, they are also fascinating and compelling literature in their own right.

## LEGENDS

The first pieces presented in this book, *Legends* (*Narraciones*), are Lorca's only surviving experiments in what, for lack of a better term, can be called poetic fiction. Though never published by the author in collected form, there is sufficient continuity between one piece and another—in violent imagery, theme, style, and the use of black humor—to consider them as an integrated group of texts. In addition, Lorca clearly viewed them this way as he gave them the collective, albeit somewhat enigmatic, title of *Narraciones*. While the term "narraciones" is usually translated as "narrations" or "accounts," it can also be used to signify "legendary tales." Given the content of the pieces, I have therefore chosen the less obvious but more resonant equivalent of *Legends*.

The opening legend, "Santa Lucía and San Lázaro," written in 1927, the longest and most sustained of the tales, was very likely inspired by Salvador Dalí's prose poem, "San Sebastián." According to Ian Gibson, Lorca's biographer, Dalí's work completely overwhelmed Lorca, and opened a major new direction in his own work, namely that of allowing the unconscious to provide the inspiration for a poetic narrative. "Santa Lucía and San Lázaro," however, goes beyond Dalí's intent, which was to create a totally subjective meditation on art and aesthetic values. Unlike Dalí's prose poem, Lorca's is not in the least didactic. It simply uses the irrational unconscious for artistic ends, without blatantly calling attention to it. Furthermore, Lorca's legend has an identifiable story line and is a far more ambitious work, for while it makes use of nonlogic, it also exploits traditional religious imagery and iconography. It is also considerably more personal and psychologically unnerving than is Dalí's.

Although "Santa Lucía and San Lázaro" is essentially the story of a traveller in a strange city, Lorca deftly exploits in it the sense of unfamiliarity any tourist has felt on alien terrain by turning commonplace bewilderment into a foreboding feeling of inner disintegration. This estrangement from the ordinary world, but most especially from the self, is revealed through powerfully metaphoric and surrealistic dream imagery in which the mundane and the miraculous uneasily coexist. In contrast to many dream narratives that revolve around the disjunction between appearance and reality, in "Santa Lucía and San Lázaro" the author refuses to admit this dichotomy. He is, in fact, relentless in his insistence that appearance *is* reality.

And what a reality! Images of the martyred Santa Lucía, who according to legend had her eyes cut out, comingle with a series of other arresting perceptions: a rain of copper bells, the skeleton of an angel, enormous spectacles and enlarged eyes, animate objects—scissors, railway rails, apples—and the appearance of a stranger with a white duster and a plaster hand.

But "Santa Lucía and San Lázaro" is not only a dazzling array of phantasmagoric effects. The perceptual disorientation is, in actuality, the outward indicator of inner distress. Returning home, the traveller discovers not the refuge expected from being in familiar surroundings, but rather a continuation of the nightmare. His suitcase is empty except for the white duster and some spectacles, "two themes of a journey." Was the stranger then himself? Were the spectacles as real as he had imagined? This twist, ironic and ominous, is the real theme of the piece: the hallucinatory city is simply the metaphoric backdrop for Lorca's description, to use Rimbaud's famous phrase, of the "derangement of the senses," of the disintegration of the individual in the modern world.

The next legend in this volume, "The History of This Rooster," was written to launch a review, *gallo* (rooster), put together by Lorca and friends in Granada in 1928. Quite different in tone and style from "Santa Lucía and San Lázaro," this legend nonetheless contains a fair amount of black humor and in its own way is also a statement on disenfranchisement, in this case from the literary establishment. Indeed, the stated purpose for composing the legend was to mount an attack on the conservative tradition in Granada. That he succeeded admirably in this aim is evident from the response to *gallo's* appearance, which he detailed in a letter to a friend:

> In Granada *gallo* has become a real scandal. Granada is a
> literary city and nothing new ever happened to it. You can't
> imagine, therefore, what an uproar *gallo* has produced. The
> edition was sold out within two days and today people are
> paying double the price for a copy. At the university there was
> a big fight between gallistas and anti-gallistas, and in the
> cafés, clubs and homes no one talks about anything else.

Unfortunately, notoriety did not bring forth patrons. With no
financing, only one more issue appeared, this one containing
Lorca's little play, "Buster Keaton's Stroll." (Number 1 had
included, along with the satiric legend, another play, also
included in this volume, "The Maiden, the Mariner and the
Student.")

In the two legends that come next in this collection,
"Beheading of the Baptist" and "Beheading of the
Innocents," Lorca uses the familiar biblical stories, and their
subsequent iconographic interpretations, to create tableaux
worthy of the Breughels or Bosch. Meticulously detailed
scenes of calculated violence, told with an almost gleeful
derision, are paraded across the page, one account of cruelty
or depravity quickly supplanting another. In "Beheading of
the Baptist" Lorca turns the event into a spectator sport, with
John the Baptist in the arena. In "Beheading of the
Innocents" Lorca's theme is that of irrational violence visited
on the heads (literally) of the powerless. Again detachment
and exceedingly dark humor dominate the powerfully vivid
descriptions of death and dismemberment, creating an
apocalyptic rendering of a world gone mad. Within ten years
of its composition, Lorca's cataclysmic vision would become
only too real in Spain and subsequently in most of Europe,
and would also claim, as callously and brutally as he depicted
it, the author himself.

The preoccupation with death was, to some extent, a theme appropriated from a long Spanish tradition. Or as Lorca himself wrote in his essay on the *Duende*, Spain is "as well as being a nation of death, a nation open to death. In all countries death is a finality. It arrives and the blinds are drawn. Not in Spain. In Spain they are opened." In part, then, Lorca is simply opening the blinds on death, but the scene he shows us is neither that of Zurbarán or El Greco. Rather it has the carnival flavor of the Spanish Good Friday processions, the incongruous, nearly comic, morbidity that arises from assigning "the dead" esteemed places in the parade of the living. It is this atmosphere that pervades nearly all of the legends, including the less graphically violent tales.

Of "Suicide in Alexandria" and "Swimmer Submerged," Lorca noted in a letter that "the two poems...correspond to my new spiritualist manner, pure disembodied emotion, detached from the control of logic, but note carefully, carefully, with a tremendous poetic logic. It is not surrealism, note carefully; the clearest consciousness illumines them. They are the first I've written. Naturally they are in prose because verse is too constrictive a ligature for them."

These two "poems in prose," and the one that follows, "Lovers Murdered by a Partridge," despite Lorca's claim that they are not surrealist works, in fact, owe a great deal to that movement. Irrational juxtaposition, perceptual impossibilities, the use of non sequiturs, and black humor, all were by 1928 common surrealist practices. The works are essentially satirical, parodies of journalese and popular romances, and although the story lines are thin, each does have some sort of recognizable plot.

"Suicide in Alexandria" is a tale of a double suicide, but unlike most popular treatments of the theme, Lorca's deprecating tone creates a kind of farce out of the event. In "Swimmer Submerged," the point of departure, as the subtitle indicates, is the newspaper gossip column. Here, death again makes an entrance, but because of the deliberate absurdity of the piece, in which society notes are interspersed with the narrator's convoluted lovelorn confession, there is absolutely no aura of tragedy. In "Lovers Murdered by a Partridge" Lorca again uses largely the monolgue form to tell the meandering and incongruous tale of a double murder, but as with the other two pieces, this legend is replete with unlikely juxtapositions and extended metaphors, but without a note of sobriety.

The last legend, "The Hen," is perhaps the least successful of the group. Published in 1934 but probably written around the same time as the other legends, it is the only truly plotless tale in the collection. Although difficult to interpret precisely, it was likely intended as a comment on the outsider, of the individual who has tastes radically different from the accepted ones. Given Lorca's sexual orientation, it could in fact be a statement on the homosexual in society, but the nonsensicality of the piece nearly defeats this purpose, if this indeed was the author's intention.

In summation, one can see the *Legends* as an attempt on the part of Lorca to embrace an international avant-garde poetics, to make a radical break with what he termed "the gypsy myth." In a 1927 letter to fellow poet Jorge Guillén, he complained that as a result of the popularity of *The Gypsy Ballads* he was becoming imprisoned in the role of gypsy poet: "Gypsies are a theme. And nothing else. I can be the same poet of sewing needles or hydraulic landscapes. Besides, gypsyism associates me with an uncultured tone, with a lack of education, makes me into a *crude poet*, which you know quite well I am not. I don't want it to imprison me."

While the desire to rupture the gypsy link may have indeed provoked him to embark in a new direction, the path itself had been paved years before. Lorca had been enthralled by Lautréamont's sinister and hallucinatory *Chants de Maldoror* as early as 1918, and during the nine years between 1919 and 1928 that he spent on and off at the *Residencia de Estudiantes* in Madrid, surrealism was a major topic of conversation. Indeed, his closest friends at the time were fellow-residents, Luis Buñuel and Salvador Dalí, and while they all influenced one another, the confluence of ideas clearly flowed in a surrealist vein.

It is not surprising, therefore, to feel on reading the *Legends* that we have somehow been here before. In fact, because these pieces have largely been ignored, the familiarity with the themes, techniques, and imagery comes from later developments, for example, from Lorca's own *Poet in New York*, or from such surrealist hallmarks as the Buñuel-Dalí 1929 collaboration, *Un Chien Andalou*, whose androgynous, impotent protagonist, according to Ian Gibson, was based on Lorca. Although Buñuel denied it, the poet certainly thought this to be the case, seeing himself as the "Andalusian dog" of the title, an epithet often used by Buñuel in referring to Lorca. The unflattering characterization caused Lorca a fair amount of pain as he felt betrayed by both his friends. At the same time, despite Buñuel's rather vehement, often homophobic denunciations of Lorca during that period, it is also clear that Buñuel was still inspired by the poet and his work. This is not the place to remark in detail on specific affinities, but it is not hard to see in the opening slit-eyeball image of that famous film an echo of "Santa Lucía and San Lázaro," or to note that the predominant themes of isolation and dehumanization have distinct counterparts in the *Legends*.

With these pieces Lorca was perfecting a style, trying out a variety of techniques, allowing the surrealist movement to inform, to liberate him from logic. In the end, however, as is the case with all great artists, Lorca made the avant-garde his own, went on to play a crucial role in creating an original modernism.

## LITTLE THEATER

Of the three short plays collected by Lorca under the title *Little Theater*, "Buster Keaton's Stroll" is the earliest (1925) and the most experimental. Like the *Legends*, it has at least some of its roots in his association with Dalí and Buñuel, particularly the latter, who first introduced Keaton's films to the students at the *Residencia*, and who was one of the first to expound on the possibilities of surrealist cinema. The play, in fact, is far more indebted to surrealism than to the American cinema, although to be sure Lorca was hardly the only one to see in Keaton the consummate tragic-comic hero. (Samuel Beckett's haunting screenplay, *Film*, written especially for Keaton, comes readily to mind.)

Despite Lorca's appropriation of Buster Keaton, it seems unlikely that his intent here was to write a film script, though it has a cinematic feeling. He employs the language of the cinema and visual effects play a major role, yet the play is also a verbal tour de force. His frequently long, lyrical and meditative "directions," for instance, are most often unfilmable. What is going on here is that Lorca is using both Keaton, and the cinematic overtones associated with him, as a vehicle for imagistic invention along surrealist lines. In short, he is counting on his readers to recognize typical Keatonian elements, so that the transformation of stock character and situation becomes even more startling.

The opening scene, for instance, provides a good clue to Lorca's intent. As the play opens, the familiar Buster of the movies strolls onto the stage, with four children in tow. His next act, however, deliberately destroys our expectations, for Buster, rather than taking a pratfall or becoming a comic victim, commits an *acte gratuit*: he slays the little ones. This is not the stuff of Hollywood, but of Buñuel, and of Lorca.

As the action progresses, a further series of bizarre encounters overtakes the hero, with slapstick stretched to the extreme, until Lorca arrives at what is a major theme in all three of these plays: repressed sexuality. The theme develops almost from the beginning where Lorca, again using the stock cinematic reference, portrays Buster, despite his murderous act, as an innocent. This allows him to set up the contrasting, and for 1925, fairly reversed roles of the male as prey to aggressive female sexuality.

If "Buster Keaton's Stroll" anticipates Buñuel's cinema, "The Maiden, the Mariner and the Student," written in late-1927 or 1928, looks forward to Lorca's own more highly developed drama, particularly the tragicomedy *If Five Years Pass* and his last play, *The House of Bernarda Alba*.

Far less indebted to surrealism than "Buster Keaton's Stroll," the story line, which might have had its origins in Lorca's poem from *The Gypsy Ballads*, "La monja gitana" ("The Gypsy Nun"), is fairly straightforward: A young woman sitting on her balcony is courted, first by a sailor and then by a student. Although she willingly plays the part of the seductress, in the end she allows neither to enter the house. Her concern, it seems, is not so much with propriety, but simply with incurring the wrath of her mother.

The theme, of course, is familiar—subverted sexuality— but the treatment in "The Maiden, the Mariner and the

Student" is largely devoid of other complications, nuances, or psychological drama. For this reason, perhaps, the play seems less evolved than many of Lorca's others. This is not to imply that "The Maiden, the Mariner and the Student" is without interest; in fact, it is a highly-charged piece, with sharp dialogue, and a definite eroticism lurking behind the often farcical facade.

Of equal interest is Lorca's introduction here of what will become a central preoccupation in many later works, most notably in *If Five Years Pass*, the concept of passing time. Like the theme of ambiguous sexuality, however, Lorca will barely develop the notion here. This is a transitional piece in which one can see the poet making an intriguing introduction to some major thematic and conceptual innovations. Working with the substantive, lyrical elements from "The Gypsy Nun," he has transformed and expanded the character and the situation, and has embarked on creating a viable drama. And while the development is sparse here, one can see the broad origins of later achievements. In the tension between mother and daughters in *The House of Bernarda Alba*, for example, one can hear echoes of dialogue or situation that hark back to this early dramatic experiment.

The last play in this collection, "Chimera," is quite simply, a little gem. In just a few pages Lorca has managed to create a full-blown drama that engages our sympathies and our imagination. Written for the third issue of *gallo* in 1928 (which never appeared), the play is essentially about a man going off on a trip, leaving at home his wife and five children. Lorca, however, has crammed far more than that into the drama's single scene, has created a memorable, haunting portrayal of stifled emotions. But the bottled sentiments here are not, as usual, those of rage; instead it is love that cannot be expressed openly. The children, for example, cannot tell their father directly what gifts they want; the wife cannot tell her husband that she loves him; the husband/father can only express impatience about getting under way. But there is no bathos here, no wallowing in feeling; and for that it is all the more powerful, all the more compelling.

Although the three plays that make up *The Little Theater* are quite different from one another in style and dramatic effect, they can all be seen as important milestones in Lorca's development as a playwright. Markedly distinct from his first produced play, *Mariana Pineda*, an historical verse drama, these works reflect definite new directions that Lorca would follow, enhance, and realize over the next few years. The sadistic surrealism and preoccupation with homsexuality in "Buster Keaton's Stroll" would not only provide a blueprint for Buñuel, but also prove fertile for Lorca in plays such as *The Public*. "The Maiden, the Mariner and the Student" is really a kind of warm-up exercise for dramas as decidedly different as *If Five Years Pass* and *The House of Bernarda Alba*. "Chimera" too foreshadows Lorca's use of sentiment, but not sentimentality, in the poignant and masterful tragedies, *Yerma* and *Blood Wedding*. In retrospect, *The Little Theater* can be seen as Lorca's theatrical apprenticeship, but to overlook the very substantial qualities of each of these works would be to risk missing some highly authentic, lyrical, and original drama.

Through *Legends* and *The Little Theater* blows a new wind, a wind that can be characterized as that of Lorca's beloved *Duende*, "a power not a construct, a struggle and not a concept." It is precisely that force that empowers the pieces and gives them their inventiveness. Lorca's own words on the *Duende* are perhaps the best illumination of what the works in this volume, and his achievements in general, best exemplify: "Through the empty arch a wind of the mind enters that blows insistently over the heads of the dead, in search of new landscapes and arcane accents, a wind smelling of child's spittle, of trampled grass, and of a Medusa's veil that trumpets the continual baptism of newly-created things."

Christopher Sawyer-Lauçanno
*Cambridge, October, 1990*

*A Note on the Text*
In making this translation I have followed, with a few minor exceptions, the authoritative Aguilar edition of Lorca's *Obras Completas*.

# LEGENDS

# SANTA LUCÍA AND SAN LÁZARO

*for Sebastià Gasch*

At midnight I arrived in the city. The frost danced on one foot. "A girl can be brunette, she can be blonde, but she can't be blind." This is what the proprietor at the inn told a man brutally sectioned in two by a waistband. The eyes of a mule, sleeping on the threshold, threatened me like two fists of jet.

"I want your best room."

"We've got one."

"Well then, let's go."

The room had a mirror. I, half a comb in my pocket: "I like it." (I saw my "I like it" in the green mirror.) The innkeeper shut the door. Then, with my back turned to the little frozen quicksilver field, I exclaimed again: "I like it." Below the mule snorted. That is to say, he opened the sunflower of his mouth.

There was nothing to do but get in bed. I lay down. But I took the precaution of leaving open the shutters, because there is nothing more beautiful than to see one star surprised and fixed within the window frame. One. The others must be forgotten.

Tonight I have an irregular and capricious sky. The stars group together and extend themselves in the glass, like signs and figures in a Japanese landscape.

While I slept, the exquisite minuet of goodnights got lost in the streets.

With the new sun I turned my gray suit out to the humid silver air. The spring day was like a languishing hand on a cushion. In the street, people came and went. They passed by fruit-sellers and fishmongers.

Not one bird.

While I rang my rings on the iron railing of the balcony, I looked for the city on the map and saw how it lay sleeping in the yellow between rich little veins of water. So far from the sea!

In the courtyard, the innkeeper and his wife sang a duet of thistle and violet. Their dark voices, like two moles in flight, stumbled against the walls without finding the framed exit to the sky.

Before going out into the street to take my first walk I went to greet them.

"Why did you say last night that a girl can be brunette or blonde but she cannot be blind?"

The innkeeper and his wife exchanged strange looks.

They stared at each other...equivocating. Like the child who brings the spoon full of soup to his eyes. Afterwards they broke into tears.

I did not know what to say and fled in a hurry.

On the door I read this sign: "Inn of Santa Lucía."

Santa Lucía was a beautiful maiden from Syracuse.

They paint her with two magnificent ox eyes on a tray.

She was martyred by order of the consul Pascasian, who had a silver mustache and howled like a mastiff.

Like all the saints, she plotted and resolved delicious theorems, causing the glass in the physics instruments to shatter.

She revealed in the public plaza, to the crowd's astonishment, that a thousand men and fifty pairs of oxen are powerless in the face of the luminous dove of the Holy Spirit. Her body, her large body, of crushed lead. Our Lord, with scepter and crown, surely was seated on her waist.

Santa Lucía was a tall girl, with small breasts and opulent hips. Like all wild women, she had eyes too large, virile eyes, with a disagreeable dark light. She died in a bed of flames.

It was the height of activity in the market and the strand of the day was filled with snails and ripe tomatoes. Before the miraculous facade of the cathedral I could understand perfectly how San Ramón Nonnato could cross the sea from the Balearic Islands to Barcelona mounted on his cape, and how the ancient Sun of China becomes infuriated and leaps like a cock over the musical towers made of dragon meat.

The people drank beer in the bars and did multiplication in the offices, while the + and × signs of the Jewish bank engaged the sacred image of the cross in dark combat, filled from within with saltpeter and snuffed candles. The fat cathedral bell poured over the city a rain of little copper bells that nailed the silly street cars and the nervous necks of the horses. I had forgotten my *Baedecker* and my binoculars and I began to see the city as one sees the sea from the shore.

All of the streets were filled with optical shops. From the facades great megatherium eyes looked out, terrible eyes, removed from the almond orbit that gives intensity to humans, eyes that aspired here to pass off inadvertently their monstrosity, feigning to be the eyelids of every Manuel, Eduardito and Enrique. Spectacles and smoked glass sought the enormous cut-off hand of the glove shop, a poem on the wind, that rang out, that bled, that bubbled like the head of John the Baptist.

The city's happiness had stopped moving and was like a child who had recently failed his exams. It had been happy, crowned with trills and trimmings of rush until a few hours ago. Then the sadness that loosens the electrical cables and raises the doorway tiles had invaded the streets with its imperceptible murmur the depth of a mirror. I began to cry because there is nothing more moving than the advent of new sadness speading itself over the still somewhat dense festivity, proving thereby that happiness is transparent to its base, filled with coins with holes in them.

It is the sadness, recently arrived, of the little paper books entitled "The Umbrella," "The Automobile" and "The Bicycle"; the sadness of *Black and White* of 1910; the sadness of the embroidered lace edging on the petticoat and the honed sadness of huge phonograph horns.

The optician's apprentices cleaned glasses in every size with chamois cloths and fine papers, producing the sound of a slithering serpent.

In the cathedral a solemn novena was offered for the human eyes of Santa Lucía. The exterior of things was glorified, the clean and sylphidine beauty of the skin, the delight in slender surfaces. Help was sought against the body's dark physiology, against the flame in its center and the funnels of night. Under the unadorned dome a pure glass sheet was raised, pierced in every direction by the finest golden reflections. The world of grass opposed the world of minerals. The fingernails against the heart. The God of contour, transparency, surface. With fear of the heart's throb and with a horror of gushing blood a plea was made for the tranquility of agates and the shadowless nakedness of the jellyfish.

When I entered the cathedral the lamentation of the six thousand virgins was being sung, sounding and resounding in the three vaulted arches filled with ship's rigging, waves and ropes, like the three battles of Lepanto. The eyes of the Saint stared from the tray with the cold suffering of an animal just put to the knife.

Space and distance. Vertical and horizontal. The relation between you and me. The eyes of Santa Lucía. The veins in the soles of her feet slept extended on the rosy beds, calmed by the two little stars that illuminated them from above. We leave our eyes on the surface, like aquatic flowers, and we conceal ourselves behind them while our palpitating physiology floats in the dark world.

I knelt.

The precentors were firing shots from the choir.

Meanwhile night had arrived. A brutal, sealed night, like the head of a mule with leather blinders.

In one of the exit doors the skeleton of an ancient fish was hanging; in another, the skeleton of an angel, swaying softly in the oval air which arrived from the optical shops freshly fragrant of apples and the sea shore.

I wanted to eat and asked the way to the inn.

"You are a long way from it. Don't forget that the cathedral is near the railroad station and that this inn lies to the south, farther along the river."

"I've got time to kill."

The train station was nearby.

A wide plaza, representative of a crippled emotion being dragged along by the waning moon, opened in the background, as firm as three o'clock in the morning.

Little by little, in the silence that disclosed the subtle relationship between fish, star and spectacles, the glasses of the optical shops were hiding themselves away in their little leather or nickel coffins.

He who has seen his spectacles isolated in moonlight or who has abandoned his impertinences on the beach, has understood, as have I, this delicate harmony (fish, star, spectacles) that collides on an immense white tablecloth recently bathed in champagne.

I could compose perfectly at least eight still-lifes with the eyes of Santa Lucía.

The eyes of Santa Lucía on the clouds, in the foreground, with an air of birds who have just taken flight.

The eyes of Santa Lucía in the sea, on a clock's face, on the sides of an anvil, on the great torso, just dismembered.

They can be related to the desert, to its vast, untrod surfaces, to a marble foot, to a thermometer, to an ox.

They cannot be joined to the mountains, nor to a distaff, nor to a toad, nor to cotton materials. The eyes of Santa Lucía.

Far from any heartbeat and far from any affliction. Permanent. Inactive. Without even a flutter. Seeing them flee all things wrapped in their difficult, eternal temperature. Worthy of the tray that gives them reality, and uplifted, like Venus's breasts, confronting the monocle laden with irony used by the evil enemy.

I set out anew, propelled by my gum-soled shoes.

A magnificent silence, surrounded by grand pianos on all sides, crowned me.

In the darkness, sketched with electric lights, one could easily read: "San Lázaro Station."

San Lázaro was born extremely pale. He gave off the smell of a wet sheep. When he was whipped, he spurted little sugar cubes from his mouth. He was sensitive to even the slightest sound. One time he confessed to his mother that in the early morning, just from the sound of their heartbeats alone, he could count every heart in the town.

He had a predilection for the silence of another orbit, one that dragged along fishes. Terror-struck, he bent low every time he passed under an archway. After his resurrection he invented the coffin, candles, magnesium lights and railroad stations. When he died he was as hard and laminated as a loaf of silver bread. His weary soul trailed behind him, long since deflowered by the other world, a reed in its hand.

The mail train had left at midnight.

I had to catch the express at two in the morning.

Entrances to cemeteries and platforms.

The same air, the same emptiness, the same shattered glasses.

The rails receded, throbbing in their precise geometrical perspective, dead and stretched out like the arm of Christ on the cross.

Apples, stiff with fear, fell from the shadowed roofs.

In the neighboring tailor shop scissors incessantly snipped pieces of white thread.

Cloth to cover everything from the shriveled breasts of an old woman to the crib of a newborn.

At the other end another traveler arrived. A traveler alone. He was dressed in a white summer suit with mother-ofpearl buttons and carried a duster of the same color. Under his straw hat, newly washed, shone his large, dying eyes, and between, his sharp nose.

His right hand was of white plaster and he carried, dangling from his arm, a willow basket filled with eggs.

I had no desire to say a word to him.

He seemed preoccupied, as though waiting for someone to call him. He was protected from his acute pallor by a long wispy beard, a beard that was the mourning guise for his own passage.

A realistic mortal symbol placed its nickel initials on my tie.

That night was the night of the fiesta in which all of Spain crowded the railings to watch a black bull, who stared with melancholy at the sky, rut four times in four minutes.

The traveler was in a country that agreed with him and on this night it fit his solitary perspective, that of waiting only for the break of dawn to take out after those voices that will, of necessity, call out.

The Spanish night, a night of red earth and iron nails, a barbarous night, with exposed breasts surprised by a single telescope. It pleased the frigid traveler. He liked its incredible depth, so deep the sounding is splintered, and he delighted in immersing his feet in the bed of ashes and burning sand on which he rested.

The traveler walked along the platform with the logic of a fish in the water or a fly in the air; he went back and forth without observing the long sad parallels awaiting the train.

I pitied him greatly for I knew he was hanging on a voice, and to hang on a voice is like being seated in front of the guillotine during the French Revolution.

A bullet in the back, an unexpected telegram, surprise. Until the wolf falls into the trap he isn't afraid. He enjoys the

silence and he enjoys the beating of the blood in his veins.
But to expect surprise is to convert an instant, always
fleeting, into a large purple globe that remains, filling up the
entire night.

The noise of a train came closer, jumbled sounds like a
thrashing.

I grabbed my suitcase, while the man in the white suit
looked around in all directions.

Finally, a clear voice, from an authoritative loudspeaker in
the back clamored: "Lázaro! Lázaro! Lázaro!" And the
traveler began to run meekly, unctuously, until he was lost in
the last lights of the station.

At the moment I heard the voice crying "Lázaro! Lázaro!
Lázaro!" my mouth filled up with fig marmalade.

I have been home only a few minutes.

Not surprisingly, I found my suitcase empty. Only some
spectacles and the white duster. Two themes of a journey.
Pure and isolated. The spectacles on the table carry to the
maximum their concrete design and their otherworldly
stability. The duster fainted in the chair in an eternal,
ultimate attitude, with a distance still a bit human, a distance
below zero, that of a drowned fish. The spectacles stretched
themselves toward an exact and demonstrable geometric
theorem, and the duster threw itself into the sea full of
shipwrecks and unexpected green splendor. Spectacles and a
duster. On the table and on the chair. Santa Lucía and San
Lázaro.

# THE HISTORY OF THIS ROOSTER

In 1830 Don Alhambro arrived in his native town of Granada after having spent many years in London where he had been perfecting his studies.

In London he had been overwhelmed from afar by the beauty of the city of his birth and had arrived desiring to observe it fully—even in its most intimate details.

He took a little room filled with pocket watches and took long walks from which he came back with the flowered suit, a melancholy moss-green like that which the Alhambra exudes into the air and onto the roofs. His Granadaism was so acute, that he constantly chewed myrtle leaves and observed at night the great historic brilliance that Granada sends out to all the other cities on the earth. He became, in addition, an

---

This "Legend" was written to introduce *gallo* (literally, rooster), a magazine of the arts founded by Lorca and friends in Granada in late 1927. The story appeared in its first issue in early 1928.

excellent connoisseur of water. The best and most authoritative connoisseur in this watery of the thousand waters.

He spoke of the water that tastes like violets, and like that of the Moorish queen, of that which tastes like marble and of the muddy water from the hills, that leaves its memory on metal nails and brandy.

He loved, with the false tenderness of a collector, all of Granada's magic potions, but he hated the typical, the picturesque and everything that transcended the clean or the customary.

Little by little the people became accustomed to seeing him. His enemies said that he was crazy and that he was an aficionado of cats and maps. His friends, in order to defend him in this rare see of avarice, claimed that Don Alhambro had hidden in his silk stocking forty ounces of gold.

He was a man with a panoramic heart and economic prudence.

On his blue frock coat he sported a cardboard label which had his name written in English.

Granada was at that time a legendary city, a finished poem that secretly hated all true poets. Fresh garlands of roses and mulberry trees encircled its walls. The cathedral turned out its round buttocks and advanced like a centaur between roofs full of dreams and green glass. At midnight, in the open air, on the railings and eaves, insecure oil lamps and cats protested the perfection of ponds.

All the clerks in The Lemon Shop painted their faces an exquisite shade of yellow in order to wait on shoppers. Really extraordinary things happened: two marble children were smashed with a hammer by the mayor because they begged alms with their hands full of dew.

It was Granada then, as it will always be: the least picturesque city in the world.

From the Silla de Moro Don Alhambro watched Granada asleep and noted that the city needed to be brought out of the lethargy in which it was submerged. He took note of the fact that a shout would resound over hearts and streets.

One night in June, preoccupied with this idea, he slept in the frizzled depths of an interminable film of breeze that the window projected on his head. His dreams were full of coconut hearts and bottles of rare Machaquito whisky, of horseshoe arches and great pages written in English, in which the word "Spain" gleamed with a golden brilliance.

What can I do, my Lord, to shake Granada from the magic stupor in which it lives? Granada has to be stirred up, it has to be like a bell in the hands of a charlatan; it must vibrate and be reconstructed. But how? In what way?

At this moment the forty images of King Carlos the Third, in forty different planes, surrounded Don Alhambro with the rhythmic madness of smashed mirrors: "Baa, baa, start a magazine," bleated aristocratically the magnificent curls of Carlos in profile. "Start a magazine, baa, baa." Our friend awakened, full of unexpected cold and delight. Between his teeth remained the jingling of gold and the episcopal wool of his dream went flying away from his eyes, full of missiles and French horsemen, fleeing with his anemone game bag for the skylight glass.

A rooster sang, and another sang, and another and another.

The songs, passionate and crinkling to their very tips plunged festive darts into the immense heart of Don Alhambro.

And he decided to found a magazine. First, he had the momentous apparition of Saint Gabriel, the archangel of propaganda, surrounded by enchanted roosters. A second later a single rooster rose up in front of his eyes that repeated in many different ways the name Granada.

"That's it. The emblem will be a rooster."

With this thought he turned himself to looking for a live rooster to serve as a model for the artist who would interpret it. Don Alhambro always sought perfect naturalness.

But what a great catastrophe!

At that time a cruel epidemic decimated the roosters in the city of Granada. They died by the hundreds. Their crest became the color of olives and their feathers were transformed into an almost invisible mass which took on the color of desert birds, creatures of ash. He took the trouble in the mornings to look out from the towers. The cockledoodledoos could be seen going out slowly, as in the liturgy, when the candles in the large candlestick are extinguished during the matins sung on Holy Thursday. From the Vela Tower he could see perfectly the sharp-pointed prominence of wings and hear the flapping murmur of death agonies. There had never been such a disquieting epidemic. Don Alhambro went from one anguish-filled house to another. He only found discolored feathers and open doors. In some places they said to him sadly: "We've already eaten the rooster," and he saw float in the speaker's eyes a dimunitive crest, comparable now, because of its delicateness, to an orchid.

But the worst of it was that although there had been thousands of roosters, all of Don Alhambro's efforts came to nothing. The millionaire Monsieur Meermans had recently arrived in town, and had bought up at an excellent price the existing roosters, because, while seated on a chair of heavy gold, he enjoyed eating great plates of uncooked crests with a fork encrusted with emeralds.

There was nothing else that our hero could do other than rob a rooster from the garden of this notable collector.

And this is the way he did it.

One night, when the clock generously struck all of its bells, he jumped over the door grate of the park and penetrated the avenues.

The Garden of the Martyrs was full of roosters. It was an earthly paradise worthy of Brueghel, a unique display of the glory of these singing birds.

From the cedars, the cypresses and the rose bushes, appeared bronze wings, black wings, strutting wings, live cane heads or pipe bowls. Don Alhambro picked up in a flash a sultan rooster that slept on a branch and departed joyously with his treasure.

On leaving the garden, the animal launched a midnight cockledoodledoo. A watery cockledoodledoo of mushrooms and violets, which was stifled in the sleeve of the erudite thief.

At that adventurous time Granada was divided into two great schools of embroidery. On one side, were the nuns of the Sacred Convent of Santo Domingo; on the other side was the eminent Paquita Raya. The nuns of Santa Domingo sequestered in a velvet box the two original needles of their baroque school, the two needles that had been used by the artists Sister Sacrament of Gold and Sister Visitation of Silver, to make their virginal marvels. It was that box, like the vestal flame, that inflamed the starched hearts of the novices. A permanent elixir of thread and counsel.

The art of Paquita Raya, on the other hand, was more popular, more vibrant, a republican art, needlework filled with open watermelons and hard apples. An art of exact realities and Spanish emotion. All the brunettes were on Paquita's side. All the blondes, those with hazel eyes and a small nucleus of albinos were on the side of the nuns. It must be said, though that both schools were marvelous. If the sisters of the convent triumphed by using a ton of gold on the robe for Soledad de Osuna, Paquita triumphed in Brussels with embroidery representing the Court of the Lions, in which more than five-and-a-half-million stitches were used.

There was little doubt on the part of Don Alhambro as to what direction to follow in order to realize his project. In the fervor of hurry, he threw caution to the wind and proceeded to the embroidery house, placing his weak hand on the cut hand of the door knocker.

"Who is it?"

It was a cold night, clean of clouds. The Hill of Gomeles bent downwards, filled with icy phonograph needles. It was one o'clock in the morning. The sorrows of the fountains beat in the fields of silence. Crystaline gushes fell from the roofs and wet the windows on the balconies. Its insomniacal tendency was joined to the physiological pain of water ruptured by a thread. An insomnia full of little incessant drums that drove the city night crazy.

"Who is it?"

The door was opened and Don Alhambro went up to the second floor. The whole house rustled and wept for the unknown martyrdom of the cloth pierced by needles.

Paquita Raya came out to receive him. She was dressed in a green silk gown with mutton sleeves, a tight belt, a white petticoat crimped with pliers and a corset of silver whalebone that had won the contest of the city of Reus. On her feet she had a pile of skeins and a bone punch, the dual symbols of technique and glory.

Neither Don Alhambro nor Paquita exchanged a word, but

Paquita understood perfectly what needed to be done. Filled with a suggestive delirium, she began to embroider, with her favorite needles, an admirable embossed rooster. Don Alhambro sadly seated himself. The live rooster that he held strongly by its feet flapped its wings wildly in the silence because he could feel that Paquita was taking away his spirit with each stitch.

A month went by, and a year and ten years. The staves of Christmas passed and the cardboard barrel hoop of Corpus Christi. The depressed Don Alhambro could not start his magazine. It was a shame. But in Granada the day had no more than one immense hour and this hour was used for drinking water, circumnavigating on a cane's axis, and looking at the landscape. He simply did not have enough physical time.

The struggle and sum of all his efforts came to nothing in this extraordinary land. Two and two are never four in Granada. They are always just two and two, without ever succeeding in forging anything more.

The last days of his life he didn't go out anymore. He passed the dead hours before a plan of the city, dreaming of seeing his own voice rise on the world map. His rooster was in front of his desk, a little hopeless and with the constancy of a weather vane.

And thus, surrounded by the incessant disagreeable whispers of his countrymen (not that they ever put their dissent in print), he arrived at the cistern's edge where he tasted his last water without explanation or agitation.

But his martyrdom was long. A full-length martyrdom. Granada broke into a thousand pieces before his eyes, a trifle anxious because of age.

In the time when Don Adolfo Contreras y Ponce de León was mayor he had already seen burned in the Plaza Nueva the last nymph captured in the forests of the Colina Roja. She sang like a quail and had guitar strings for hair. For several days the ground, where her feet had been immersed, was covered with violets, like confetti strewn about after a carnival.

The same morning that the project was approved to open the Gran Vía, a project that has contributed so much to deforming the character of present-day Granadans, Don Alhambro died.

Four candles.

Nobody at his burial. Yes, the swallows. A shame.

After the burial the rooster exited through the window flinging himself into the dangerous streets and a wayward life. Then he began to ask for alms from the English at the Puerta de Vino and became friends with two dwarfs who played the flute and sold candy bulls. A real come down. Then he disappeared.

When my friends decided to found this magazine they did not know what name to give it. I knew the story of Don Alhambro's rooster, but didn't dare to bring it up. Then suddenly, a few days later all the contented editors came up to my house. They brought with them an admirable rooster. It had Rolls Royce blue and colonial grey feathers with a neck all delicious Falla blue which was accentuated further on its spurs.

"Where did you get this rooster?"

"I'm the rooster of Don Alhambro!"

"Ah, go on," everybody shouted.

"I've brought myself back to life in order to come and seek

you out so that I can ascend to the title I so desire and for which I was created."

"The title that I like is *The Moor's Sigh*," I said.

"*Romeo and Juliet*," said another.

"*A Glass of Water*," repeated another little voice.

"Gentlemen, my God!" cried the rooster. "I don't ask you to share Don Alhambro's ideology; I too have changed my opinion, but because of my history, don't reject me. I won't tolerate it. Here you can't do anything without taking history into account. I'm beautiful. I announce the morning. And as an emblem I will always be indispensable."

There was a violent discussion in which the rooster pleaded his case most tenderly.

"Enough, my friends," I said energetically. "I'll take responsibility. Ascend to the title!"

We opened the balcony and the rooster ascended to the top of the title with all his feathers aflame. Already at the helm of the title, he saluted us all in an ineffable fashion. Like that of water and hyacinth. A poem by a poet who breaks a guitar over the morning sea. A dahlia in the olive grove and forest at hand. Game and lie.

We have celebrated the ascension of the rooster to the title of this magazine by embroidering on silk four bright yellow hens so that its beak might fully enjoy the zig zag fruit of the presses in the evocative dark dawn of print. While my friends applauded, I sensed touchingly the smile of Don Alhambro, that came to me wrapped in dense cotton from the trunk of a sepulcher.

Sing, rooster, rooster reborn, rooster of resistance.

Sing sure beneath your little hat of flames, because one of your hens might very well lay the golden eggs.

# THE BEHEADING OF THE BAPTIST

*for Luis Montanyá*

| The Baptist: | Ay! |
|---|---|
| The Black Team: | Ay Ay! |
| The Baptist: | Ay! Ay! |
| The Black Team: | Ay Ay! Ay! |
| The Baptist: | Ay! Ay! Ay! |
| The Black Team: | Ay Ay! Ay! Ay! |

The black team finally won. But the people were convinced that the red team should have won. The woman who had just given birth had a terrible fear of blood, but beneath the balconies blood danced slowly with a bone dyed crimson. White cloth was not allowed to exist, nor was the sweet water in the valleys. The moon's presence was intolerable, and they wished for a bull slit open, a bull beheaded with an axe swarming with great fat flies.

The planets' tremors reechoed in the flesh under the fingertips and the families grew to hate the weeping, the weeping of the crumb-gathering partridges who shut down the dance.

Ribbons had dethroned the serpents and a woman's neck made the smoke and the barber's knife possible.

| | |
|---|---|
| The Baptist: | Ay! Ay! Ay! Ay! |
| The Black Team: | Ay! Ay! Ay! |
| The Baptist: | Ay! Ay! Ay! |
| The Black Team: | Ay! Ay! |
| The Baptist: | Ay! Ay! |
| The Black Team: | Ay! |
| The Red Team (subtly appearing): | Ay! Ay! Ay! Ay! |

The red team won. In blinding triangles of flame. Kissing a child, dead, imprisoned, was necessary in order to chew that abandoned flower. Salomé had more than seven false teeth and a flask of venom. To him, to him! They have now arrived at the dungeon.

He will have to fight with the vixen and with the moon in the taverns. He will have to fight. He will have to fight.

Could it be possible that the doves that cherish their silence and the immortals might be knocking so furiously on the door? My son. My oblique-eyed son, shut the door so that no one will suspect your presence. The Hebrews are coming! They're coming! Beneath a sky of gathered cloths and counterfeit coins.

The palms of my hands hurt from holding up the spindly legs of sparrows. My son! My love! A man can survey the hills in searth of his pistol, and a barber can and must make crosses of blood on the necks of his clients, but we don't have to lean out the window.

The red team won. I told you. The shops have hurled all their scarves at the blood. At police headquarters they assure themselves that the shame has increased a thousand times a thousand.

| The Baptist: | knife |
| The Red Team: | sword sword |
| The Baptist: | knife knife |
| The Red Team: | sword sword sword |
| The Baptist: | knife knife knife |
| The Red Team: | sword sword sword sword |

They won finally with the last goal.

Beneath a sky of foot soles. The beheading was horrifying. But carried out marvelously. The sword was monstrous. In short, the flesh is ultimately always like a frog's belly. You have to go against the flesh. You have to set up sword factories so that horror can stir its intravenous forest. The beheading specialist is the enemy of emeralds. I always told you that, my son. He doesn't know about chewing gum, but he does know about the tender neck of a live partridge.

The baptist was on his knees. The beheader was a midget. But the sword was a sword. A sparkling sword, a flaming sword with cruel teeth.

An outcry from the stadium caused the cows to bellow in every stable in Palestine. The head of the celestial fighter was in the middle of the arena. The young women all had red cheeks and the young men painted their ties in the shuddering cannon of the slit jugular.

| | |
|---|---|
| The Baptist's Head: | Light! |
| The Red Team: | Blade! |
| The Baptist's Head: | Light! Light! |
| The Red Team: | Blade! Blade! |
| The Baptist's Head: | Light! Light! Light! |
| The Red Team: | Blade! Blade! Blade! Blade! |

# BEHEADING OF THE INNOCENTS

Tris, tras. Zig zag. Rig rag, milg malg. The flesh was so tender it came off in one piece. Little boys and Adam's apples newly clotted.

The warriors had millenary roots, and the sky had wigs rocked by an amphibian spirit. It was essential to close the doors. Pepito. Manolito. Enriquito. Eduardito. Jaimito. Emilito.

When the mothers went mad they wanted to build a hat factory of jasper, but they never could do anything about the cruel loss of tenderness in their leaking breasts.

They rolled up the carpets. The bee's sting facilitated the handling of the sword.

It was necessary to rustle the bones and break the river dams. A china basin was enough. But a china basin that isn't afraid of the interminable gush that has to sound for three days.

They ascended the towers and descended to the snails. A light from the clinic finally conquered the unctuous light of the hospital. Now it was possible to operate with all guarantees. Iodine and violet, cotton and silver of another world. Come on in! Some people threw themselves from the towers to the patios; other desperate individuals nailed tacks into their knees. The morning light was sharp-edged and the oily wind caused the least expected wound.

Jorgito, Alvarito, Guillermito, Leopoldito, Julito, Joseito, Luisito. Innocents. The steel needs heat to produce the nebulae. Let's go to the untiring blade. It's better to be a jellyfish and float than to be a child. Oh happy beheading! The logical function of blood without light that bleeds against its walls.

They came through the most distant streets. Each dog carried a little foot in its mouth. The mad pianist gathered up rosy fingernails to make an unemotional piano, and the faithful gaped at the severed necks.

It is necessary to round up two hundred little boys and bring them for beheading. Only in this way can the autonomy of the wood lily be assured.

Come! Come! Here is my most tender son, my son with the easy neck. In the landing of the stairway you will be able to behead him easily.

They say that they are inventing the electric knife to revitalize the operation.

Do you remember the nightingale with two broken legs? It was among the insects, creators of tremors and salivation. Points of a needle. And spider trails across the constellations. It brings a real smile to think of how cold the water is. Cold water for the sand, cold skies and the backsides of alligators. Here in the streets run the most hidden, the most palatable, who dye their teeth and make their fingernails pallid. Blood. With all the force of its "B."

If we meditate on it and are filled with true pity, we will carry out beheadings as one of the greatest acts of mercy. Mercy for the blind blood that, following the natural laws, wants to empty out into the sea. It did not have, at least, one voice. The Hebrew leader crossed the square to calm the multitude.

At six in the evening there were no more than six little boys left to behead. The hourglasses continued to bleed but the wounds were all dry.

All the blood had crystalized by the time they began to light the lanterns. There was never another night in the whole world to equal it. A night of glass and little ice-cold hands.

Breasts filled up with useless milk.

The maternal milk and the moon endured the battle against the triumphant blood. But the blood had already been seized by the marbles and there nailed down its last mad roots.

## SUICIDE IN ALEXANDRIA

### 13 & 22

When they placed the severed head on the office table, all
the glass in the city shattered. "It will be necessary to calm
these roses," said the old woman. An automobile went by and
it was a 13. Another automobile went by and it was a 22. A
shop went by and it was a 13. A kilometer went by and it was
a 22. The situation had become insupportable. It had to be
broken off forever.

### 12 & 21

After the terrible ceremony everybody climbed up to the top
leaf of the thistle, but the ant was so large, so large, that it
had to stay on the ground with the hammer and the threaded
needle's eye.

## 11 & 20

They were then off in an automobile. They wanted to kill themselves in order to become an example and to eliminate the possibility of a single canoe getting close to the shore.

## 10 & 19

They broke the partitions and waved their handkerchiefs. Genevieve! Genevieve! It was night and called for a set of teeth and the whip.

## 9 & 18

There being no other way, they killed themselves. That is to say, we killed ourselves. My dearest! My love! The Eiffel Tower is pretty, and the somber Thames as well. If we go to Lord Butown's house he will give us a lobster head and a little smoke ring. But we're not going to this Chilean's house.

## 8 & 17

There's no other way now. Kiss me without tearing my tie. Kiss me. Kiss me.

## 7 & 16

I, a child, and you, beloved of the sea. We recognize that the right cheek is a world without norms and astronomy a soap sliver.

## 6 & 15

Goodbye. Help! Love, my love! Now we'll die together. For the love of God finish this poem.

## 5 & 14
## 4 & 13

When the moment arrived we saw the lovers in each other's arms in the waves.

## 3 & 12
## 2 & 11
## 1 & 10

An enormous wave violently swept over the docks and covered the boats. Only a muted voice could be heard crying out from among the fish.

9
8
7
6
5
4
3
2
1
0

We'll never forget, those who summer on the Alexandrine beach, that emotional love scene that clawed tears from all our eyes.

## SWIMMER SUBMERGED
### Little Homage to a Society Columnist

I loved two women who didn't love me, but nonetheless I didn't want to behead my favorite dog. Doesn't it seem to you, Countess, that my attitude is one of the purest that can be adopted?

Now I know what it is to say goodbye forever. The daily embrace has the breeze of molluscs.

This last embrace of my love was so perfect that the people secretly closed off their balconies. Don't make me talk to you, Countess. I am in love with a woman who has half of her body in the northern snows. A woman who is a friend to dogs but fundamentally my enemy.

I never could kiss her with enjoyment. She turned out the lights or dissolved in a whisky flask. I was not then an aficionado of English gin. Imagine, my friend, the quality of my suffering.

One night the devil did horrible things with my shoes. It was three in the morning. I had a scalpel across my throat and she had a large silk handkerchief. I lie. It was a horse's tail. The tail of an invisible horse that had dragged me along. Countess: It's good you're squeezing my hand.

We began to discuss it. I made a deep scratch in my forehead, and she, with great dexterity, parted the glass pane in her cheek. We then held one another.

You already know the rest.

The orchestra in the distance fought dramatically with flying ants.

Madame Barthou made the night irresistible with her diseased diamonds from Cairo, and the violet dress of Olga Montcha denounced, more palpably each minute, her love for the dead czar.

Margarita Gross and the most Spanish Lola Cabeza de Vaca had managed to count more than a thousand waves but with no result.

On the French coast the murderers of mariners and those who steal the fishermen's salt began to sing.

Countess: That ultimate embrace had three tempos and evolved marvelously.

Since then I left behind the old literature that I had cultivated with such great success.

It is essential to break with everything so that dogmas can purify themselves and standards become earth shaking.

Elephants must have partridge eyes and partridges unicorn hooves.

I have learned all of these things from an embrace and also for this love my silk jacket has been slashed.

Do you not hear that American waltz? In Vienna there are too many almond ices and too much intellectualism. The American waltz is as perfect as a naval academy. Would you like a whirl on the dance floor?

The next morning the Countess of X was found on the beach with a wormwood fork stuck in her neck. Her death must have been instantaneous. In the sand they found a little blood-stained piece of paper that said: "Since you can't become a dove, you are better off dead."

The police rode their bicycles up and down the dunes.

It was determined that the countess loved to swim and that this was the cause of death.

We can positively affirm that the name of her marvelous assassin was never learned.

# LOVERS MURDERED BY A PARTRIDGE
## (Homage to Guy de Maupassant)

"*The two of them wanted it,*" his mother told me.

"Both of them? That's not possible, madame," I said. You are too temperamental, and at your age you already know why pins fall from dew.

"Be quiet, Luciano. Be quiet. No, no, Luciano, no."

"To resist this name I would have to bottle up the pain of my memories. And you think that this small set of teeth and this child's hand forgotten in the waves can console me in my sadness? *The two of them wanted it,*" his cousin told me. The two of them. I began to look out at the sea and understood everything.

"Could it be possible that the beak of this cruel dove that has the heart of an elephant engenders the lunar pallor of that transatlantic liner steaming away?

"Do I have to make use various times of my spoon to defend myself from the wolves? Not any of it is my fault. You know that. My God! I'm crying."

"The two of them wanted it," I said. The two of them.

An apple will always be a lover, but a lover can never ever be an apple.

For this they died. For this. With twenty rivers and a single slit-throated winter.

"It was very simple. They made love on top of all the museums. Right hand with left hand. Left hand with right hand. Right foot with right foot. Left foot with a cloud. Hair with the sole of a foot. The sole of a foot with a left cheek. Oh that left cheek! Oh northwester with little boats and quicksilver ants! Pass me the handkerchief, Genevieve, I'm going to cry. I'm going to cry until my eyes shoot forth an immortal multitude. They went to bed. There was never a sight more tender. Did you hear me? They went to bed. Left thigh with left forearm. Eyes closed with fingernails open. The waist with the neck and with the beach. And the four ears were four angels in a snow hut. They loved each other. They made love. Despite the law of gravity. The difference existing between a rose thorn and a star is so singular. When they discovered this they set out for the countryside. They made love. My God! They made love under the eyes of chemists. Back with earth, earth with anise. The moon with a shoulder asleep and waists intertwining with the sound of glass. I saw her cheeks tremble when the professors from the university brought honey and vinegar on a small sponge. Many times they had to separate the dogs that howled from beds whitened with ivy. But they made love.

"It was a man and a woman, or a man and a little piece of earth, an elephant and a child, a child and a reed. There were two pale workmen and a nickel leg. They were the boatmen. Yes, they were the boatmen of Guadiana, who encircled with their oars all the roses in the world.

"The old sailor spit out the tobacco from his mouth and gave a great yell to frighten off the sea gulls. But by now it was already too late.

"It happened. It had to happen. When the women in mourning arrived at the governor's house, he was calmly eating green almonds and fresh fish on an exquisite gold plate. It was preferable not to talk with him.

"In the Azores Islands. I can barely cry. I sent two telegrams. But unfortunately, it was already late. I only know to say to you that some children, passing by the edge of the forest saw a partridge that spit out a thread of blood from its beak.

"And this is the cause, dear captain, of my strange melancholy."

## THE HEN
### (A Story for Foolish Children)

There was a little girl who was an idiot. I said an idiot. But
she was even more of an idiot than that. A mosquito bit her
and she took off running. A wasp stung her and she took off
running. A bat bit her and she took off running.

All hens are afraid of foxes. But this hen wanted to be
devoured by them. And so it was that the hen was an idiot.
She was not a hen. She was an idiot.

On winter nights the moon in the villages slapped the
hens viciously. The slaps were so hard they could be heard in
the streets. It gave them lots of laughs. The priests couldn't
ever understand the reason for these slaps, but God did. And
so did the hens. It will demonstrate, so that you all might
know, that God is a great LIVING mountain. He has a skin
of flies, and on top of that a skin of wasps, and on top of that
a skin of swallows, and on top of that a skin of lizards, and on
top of that a skin of worms and on top of that a skin of men
and on top of that a skin of leopards and all. Do you see them

all? Well everything, and also a skin of hens. This is what our friend didn't know.

It makes one laugh to think how amiable hens are! They all have crests. They all have tails. They all lay eggs. What were you going to say to me?

The idiot hen hated eggs. She liked roosters, certainly, just as people enjoy having their right hands pierced by thorns or delight in the initiation of a pin prick. But she hated her own egg. Nonetheless, there is nothing more beautiful than an egg.

Recently taken from the corn stalks, still warm, it is perfection for the mouth, the eyelid and the earlobe. The warm cheek of a new corpse. It is the face. Don't you understand? I do. The Japanese stories talk about it and some unlettered women also know.

I don't want to defend the sparse beauty of an egg, but now that everyone boasts of beauty in the mirror and about happiness from rolling in the grass, it's best that I defend an egg against an idiot hen.

I am going to tell you: A hen, the friend of man.

One night the moon was slapping around the hens. The sea and the roofs and the coal sheds all had the same light. A light where the moths might have received everyone's arrows. Nobody slept. The hens couldn't either. Their crests were frost-bound and the lice rang their electric bells in the interval between slaps.

One rooster finally decided.

The idiot hen defended herself.

The rooster danced three times, but the roosters did not know how to thread the needles very well.

The tower bells rang because they had to ring, and the river beds and the runners and the golfers turned mulberry red three times and clanged like bells. The fight began.

Ready rooster. Idiot hen. Ready hen. Idiot rooster. Both of them ready. The two idiots. Ready rooster and idiot hen.

They fought, they fought, they fought. All night. And ten nights. And twenty. And a year. And ten years. And forever.

# PLAYS FROM
# THE LITTLE THEATER

# BUSTER KEATON'S STROLL

## CAST OF CHARACTERS

| | | |
|---|---|---|
| Buster Keaton | An owl | An American Woman |
| A rooster | A black man | A young woman |

ROOSTER: Cockledoodledoo!

*(Buster Keaton enters hand in hand with his four children.)*

BUSTER KEATON: *(He takes out a wooden dagger and kills them.)* My poor children!

ROOSTER: Cockledoodledoo!

BUSTER KEATON: (*Counting the bodies on the ground*) One, two, three and four. (*He grabs a bicycle and leaves.*)

(*Among old gum tires and gasoline cans a black man eats his straw hat.*)

BUSTER KEATON: What a beautiful afternoon!

(*A parrot flutters in the neutral sky.*)

BUSTER KEATON: Such pleasure to take the air on a bicycle.

OWL: Hoo, Hoo, Hoo, Hoo.

BUSTER KEATON: The birds sing so splendidly.

OWL: Hooooooooooo.

BUSTER KEATON: It's thrilling.

(*Pause. Buster Keaton ineffably crosses the bulrushes and little field of rye. The landscape recedes behind the bicycle wheels. The bicycle has only one dimension. It can enter the books and extend itself into the bread oven. Buster Keaton's bicycle does not have a caramel saddle or sugar pedals like those that villains would want. It is just an ordinary bicycle, except for being uniquely imbued with innocence. Adam and Eve would run away frightened if they were to see a glass full of water, but would caress Keaton's bicycle.*)

BUSTER KEATON: Oh love! Love!

*(Buster Keaton falls to the ground. The bicycle escapes him. It runs after two giant gray butterflies, crazily flying a half-millimeter off the ground.)*

BUSTER KEATON: *(Getting up)* I don't want to say anything. What am I going to say?

A VOICE: Simpleton.

*(He continues walking. His eyes, immense and sad like those of a beast just born, dream of irises, angels and silk sashes. Glass-bottom eyes. Eyes of a stupid child. Terribly ugly. Terribly beautiful. Eyes of an ostrich. Human eyes in the sure equilibrium of melancholy. In the distance he sees Philadelphia. Although the city's inhabitants already know that the old poem of the Singer sewing machine can encircle the grand greenhouse roses of winter, they will never be able to comprehend the subtle poetic difference existing between a cup of hot tea and a cup of cold tea. Philadelphia shines in the distance.)*

BUSTER KEATON: This is a garden.

*(An American woman with celluloid eyes comes through the grass.)*

AMERICAN WOMAN: Good afternoon.

*(Buster Keaton smiles and in a "close-up" looks over the woman's shoes. Oh what shoes! We can't allow those shoes. It took three crocodile hides to make them.)*

AMERICAN WOMAN: Do you have a sword adorned with myrtle leaves?

(*Buster Keaton shrugs his shoulders and lifts his right foot.*)

AMERICAN WOMAN: Do you have a ring with a poison stone?

(*Buster Keaton slowly shuts his eyes and lifts his left foot.*)

AMERICAN WOMAN: Well then?

(*Four seraphim with wings of gauze celestially dance among the flowers. The young ladies of the city play the piano as if they were riding a bicycle. The waltz, the moon, and the canoes stir the precious heart of our friend. With great surprise to all, autumn has invaded the garden, like water on a lump of sugar.*)

BUSTER KEATON: (*Sighing*) I would like to be a swan. But even though I would like to be, I cannot. Because...Where would I leave my hat? Where my wing-collar and my moire tie? What a disgrace!

(*A wasp-waisted young woman with a high bodice and stiff collar enters riding a bicycle. She has a nightingale's head.*)

YOUNG WOMAN: Whom do I have the honor to greet?

BUSTER KEATON: (*bowing*) Buster Keaton.

(*The young woman faints and falls off the bicycle. Her striped legs tremble on the grass like two dying zebras. A gramophone announces at a thousand shows at once: "In America there are nightingales."*)

BUSTER KEATON: *(Kneeling)* Miss Eleonora. Forgive me for not having been. Miss! *(Lower)* Miss! *(Even lower)* Miss! *(He kisses her.)*

*Against the Philadelphia skyline shine the policemen's flashing stars.)*

# THE MAIDEN, THE MARINER
# AND THE STUDENT

## CAST OF CHARACTERS

| | | |
|---|---|---|
| The Maiden | The Mariner | The Student |
| An Old Woman | The Mother | |

*(A Balcony)*

OLD WOMAN: *(in the street)* Snaaaaaails. Cooked with peppermint, saffron and laurel leaves.

MAIDEN: Little snails from the country. Heaped up in the basket like that they look like some ancient Chinese city.

OLD WOMAN: This old woman sells them. They are great and dark. Four of these would make a snake. What snails! My God, what snails!

MAIDEN: Leave me to my embroidery. My pillow cases do not have my initials on them and this makes me very afraid. What girl in the world doesn't have her clothes marked?

OLD WOMAN: What is your name?

MAIDEN: I embroider my clothes with all of the letters of the alphabet.

OLD WOMAN: What for?

MAIDEN: So that the man who will be with me may call me anything he wishes.

OLD WOMAN: Then you are a shameless creature.

MAIDEN: (lowering her eyes) Yes.

OLD WOMAN: So you can be named María, Rosa, Trinidad? Segismunda?

MAIDEN: And more and more.

OLD WOMAN: Eustaquia? Dorotea? Jenara?

MAIDEN: And more, more, more.

(The maiden lifts up the palms of her hands, pallid from watching the silk and the markers. The old woman flees along the wall toward her Siberia of dark rags and the dying basket brimming with bits of alms bread.)

MAIDEN: A, B, C, D, E, F, G, H, I, J, K, L, M, N. That's fine. I'm going to close off the balcony. Behind the windows I'll continue with my embroidery.

(*Pause*)

THE MOTHER: (*From within*) My daughter, my daughter. Are you crying?

MAIDEN: No. It's started to rain.

(*A canoe car, filled with flags crosses the bay, leaving its stammering song in the wake. The rain caps the city with a professor's mortar board. In the taverns of the port, the mariner's great binge begins.*)

MAIDEN: (*Singing*)
A, B, C, D.
Which letter will stay with me?
Mariner begins with M
And student starts with S
A, B, C, D.

MARINER: (*Entering*) I.

MAIDEN: You?

MARINER: A boat is such a paltry thing.

MAIDEN: I'll put flags and candies on it.

MARINER: If the captain wants.

*(Pause)*

MAIDEN: *(Pained)* A boat is such a paltry thing.

MARINER: I'll fill it with embroidered lace.

MAIDEN: If my mother allows me.

MARINER: Stand up.

MAIDEN: What for?

MARINER: So that I can see you.

MAIDEN: *(She gets up.)* Here I am.

MARINER: What beautiful thighs you have.

MAIDEN: I've ridden a bicycle ever since I was a child.

MARINER: And I a dolphin.

MAIDEN: You, too, are beautiful.

MARINER: When I'm naked.

MAIDEN: What do you know how to do?

MARINER: Row.

*(The mariner plays a dusty and tired accordion, as in a 17th-century painting.)*

STUDENT: *(Entering)* It goes too quickly.

MAIDEN: What goes too quickly?

STUDENT: The century.

MAIDEN: You are terrified.

STUDENT: I am escaping.

MAIDEN: From whom?

STUDENT: From the coming year.

MAIDEN: Haven't you seen my face?

STUDENT: That's the reason that I stopped.

MAIDEN: You aren't very dark.

STUDENT: That's because I live at night.

MAIDEN: What do you want?

STUDENT: Give me some water.

MAIDEN: We don't have a well.

STUDENT: Well—I'm dying of thirst.

MAIDEN: I'll give you milk from my breasts.

STUDENT: *(Aflame)* Sweeten my mouth.

MAIDEN: But I'm a maiden.

STUDENT: If you will throw me down a ladder, I'll spend this night with you.

MAIDEN: You are pale and will be very cold.

STUDENT: My arms are strong.

MAIDEN: I will let you if my mother wishes.

STUDENT: Come on.

MAIDEN: No.

STUDENT: Why not?

MAIDEN: Well, because...

STUDENT: Come on...

MAIDEN: No.

*(Around the moon revolves a wheel of dark brigantines. Three sirens splashing in the waves slyly beckon the soldiers from the coast. The maiden, on the balcony, thinks of leaping from the letter Z and throwing herself into the abyss. Emilio Prados and Manolito Altolaguirre, sprinkled with flour for fear of the sea, gently remove her from the balcony.)*

# CHIMERA

## CAST OF CHARACTERS

Enrique Old Man Voices
Wife Little Girl Little Boy

*(A Doorway)*

ENRIQUE: Goodbye.

SIX VOICES: *(From within)* Goodbye.

ENRIQUE: I will be gone a long time in the mountains.

VOICE: A squirrel.

ENRIQUE: Yes. A squirrel for you, and also five birds like no child has ever had before.

VOICE: No, I want a lizard.

VOICE: And I, a mole.

ENRIQUE: You children are all very different. but I'll fulfill each of your requests.

OLD MAN: Very different.

ENRIQUE: What did you say?

OLD MAN: Can I carry your bags?

ENRIQUE: No. (*The children's laughter is heard.*)

OLD MAN: Are they your children?

ENRIQUE: All six of them.

OLD MAN: I've known their mother, your wife, for a long time. I was a coach driver in her house, but to tell you the truth, I'm now little better than a beggar. It's the horses. Ha, ha, ha! Nobody knows how much horses frighten me. May lightning blind them all! Driving a coach is very difficult. Oh, it's incredibly difficult. If you aren't afraid, you don't know them fully. And if you don't know them fully, you aren't afraid. Oh. Those damned horses!

ENRIQUE: (*Grabbing his bags*) Leave me alone.

OLD MAN: No, no. For just a pittance, for the smallest coins you have, I'll take them for you. Your wife will appreciate it. She wasn't afraid of horses. She's happy.

ENRIQUE: Let's go quickly. I have to catch the six o'clock train.

OLD MAN: Ah, the train. That's another matter. The train is a stupidity. Even if I should live to be a hundred, I wouldn't be afraid of the train. The train isn't alive. It passes by and then is gone. But the horses...Look.

WIFE: (*In the window*) My Enrique. Enrique. Don't forget to write. Don't forget me.

OLD MAN: Oh, that girl. (*He laughs.*) Do you remember how he used to scale that mud wall and climb up the trees just to be able to see you?

WIFE: I'll remember it until the day I die.

ENRIQUE: So will I.

WIFE: I'll wait for you. Goodbye.

ENRIQUE: Goodbye.

OLD MAN: Don't be miserable. She's your wife and she loves you. You love her. Don't be miserable.

ENRIQUE: Yes, it's true. But this absence is weighing on me.

OLD MAN: Other things are worse. It is worse that

everything keeps on moving and that the river gurgles. A cyclone would be much worse.

ENRIQUE: I'm not in the mood for jokes. You're always like this.

OLD MAN: Ha, ha, ha! Everybody, and you more than anyone, think that the importance of a cyclone lies in the destruction it causes. I believe the exact opposite. The importance of a cyclone...

ENRIQUE: (Irritated) Come on! It's going to be six any minute now.

OLD MAN: Well, and the sea? In the sea...

ENRIQUE: (Furious) Let's go I said!

OLD MAN: You didn't forget anything?

ENRIQUE: I left everything in perfect order. And besides, what's it to you? The worst thing in the world is an old servant, a beggar.

VOICE 1: Papa.

VOICE 2: Papa.

VOICE 3: Papa.

VOICE 4: Papa.

VOICE 5: Papa.

VOICE 6: Papa.

OLD MAN: Your children.

ENRIQUE: My children.

LITTLE GIRL: *(In the doorway)* I don't want a squirrel. If you bring me a squirrel I won't love you. Don't bring me a squirrel. I won't want it.

VOICE: And I don't want a lizard.

VOICE: And I don't want a mole.

LITTLE GIRL: We want you to bring us back a rock collection.

VOICE: No. No. I want my mole.

VOICE: No. The mole is for me.

*(They scuffle.)*

LITTLE GIRL: Well, now the mole is going to be for me.

ENRIQUE: Enough. Content yourselves.

OLD MAN: I told you they were very different.

ENRIQUE: Yes, very different. Fortunately.

OLD MAN: How's that?

ENRIQUE: *(Firmly)* Fortunately.

OLD MAN: *(Sadly)* Fortunately.

*(They leave.)*

WIFE: *(In the window)* Goodbye.

VOICE: Goodbye.

WIFE: Come back soon.

VOICE: *(Far away)* Soon.

WIFE: He'll be well covered at night. He has four blankets
with him. But I'll be in bed alone. I will be cold. He has
marvelous eyes, but what I love most about him is his
strength. *(She undresses.)* My back hurts me a bit. Oh! If
he could only despise me. I want him to despise me...and
love me. I want to escape and have him catch me. I want
him to set me on fire...set me on fire. *(Aloud.)* Goodbye.
Goodbye. Enrique. Enrique. I love you. I see you growing
small. You leap over the rocks. Small. Now I could swallow
you as if you were a new flower bud. I could swallow you,
Enrique...

LITTLE GIRL: Mama.

WIFE: Don't go out. A cold wind's blown up. I told you, no!

*(She enters. Light fades from the stage.)*

LITTLE GIRL: *(Rapidly)* Paapaaa! Paapaaa! Bring me the

squirrel. I don't want the rocks. The rocks will break my fingernails. Paapaaa.

LITTLE BOY: *(In the doorway)* He can't hear you. He can't hear you. He can't hear you.

LITTLE GIRL: Papa, I do want the squirrel. *(She bursts into tears.)* My God, I want the squirrel!

# ALSO FROM CITY LIGHTS BOOKS

POEM OF THE DEEP SONG
by Federico García Lorca
Translated by Carlos Bauer

ODE TO WALT WHITMAN
by Fedrico García Lorca
Translated by Carlos Bauer